STARLIGHT

© Julia Artis, 2023
All rights reserved. No part of this book may be reproduced or utilized in any form or by any means, electronic or mechanical, including photocopying, recording, or by any information storage and retrieval system, without permission in writing from the author.

First published in 2023
Published by Journey Together Publishing

Written by Julia Artis
Illustrated by Fuuji Takashi
Book design by Bryony van der Merwe

ISBN: 979-8-3507-0600-0 (hardcover)
ISBN: 979-8-218-13690-1 (paperback)
ISBN: 979-8-218-17134-6 (ebook)

Dedicated to

my HUSBAND Ron Artis II

and the child within
each and everyone's heart.

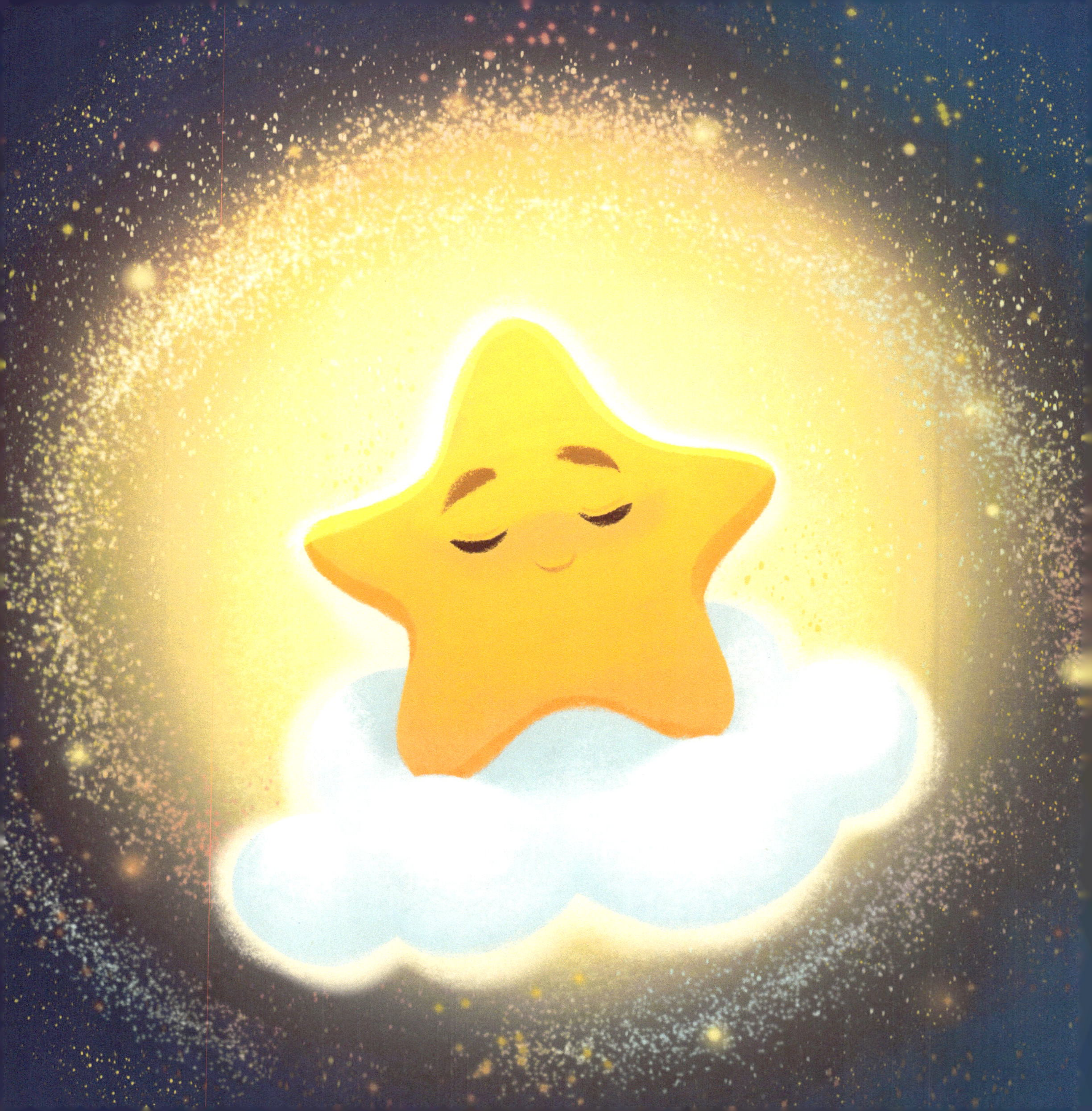

Once there was a little STAR.

Shining bright and oh so far.

But suddenly he
lost his LIGHT.
and felt LONELY
in the night.

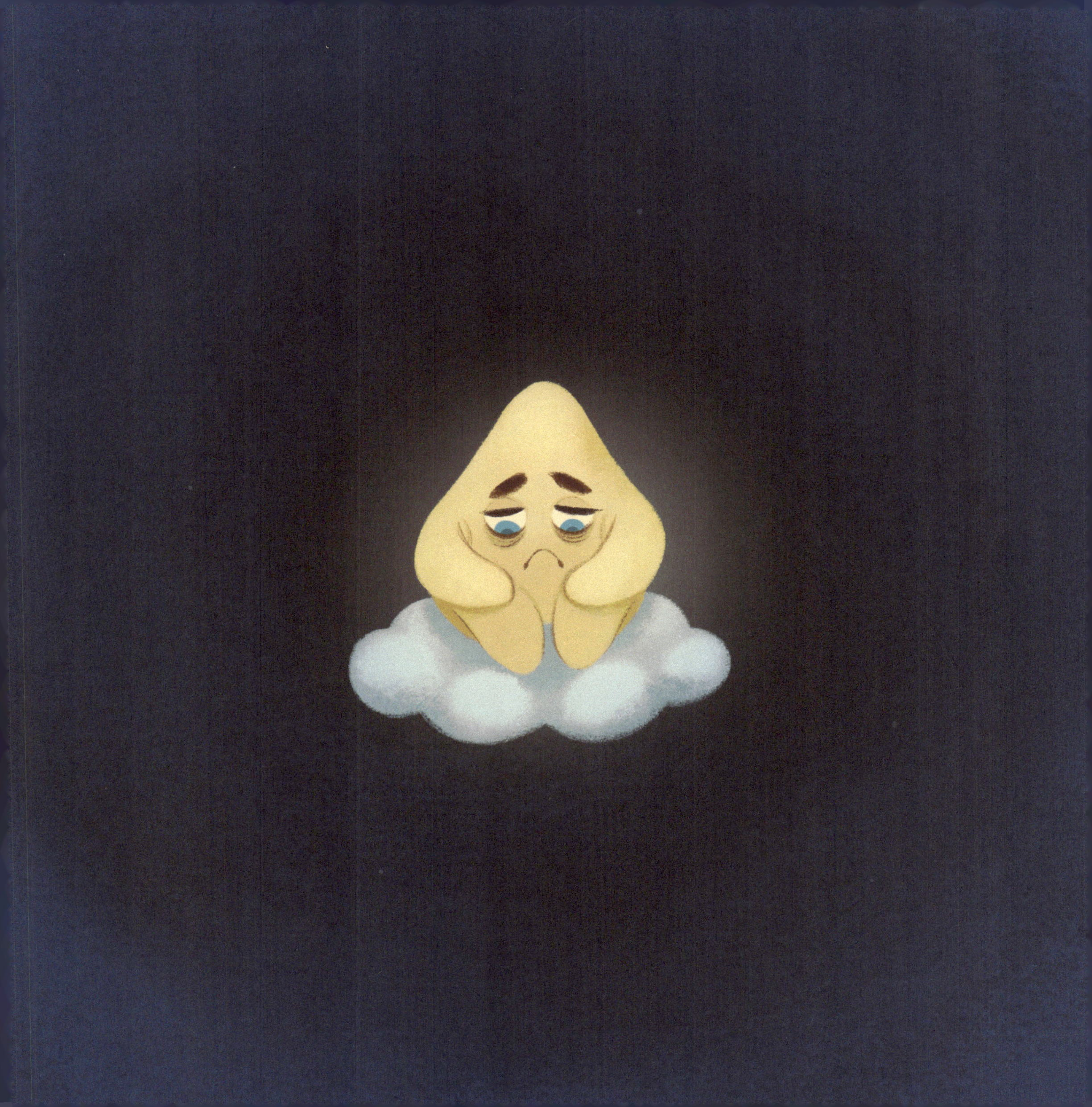

"If I find the BRIGHTEST Stars,

"I'll SHINE like them!" he said to Mars.

But the
BRIGHT ones
didn't help
him much..

felt **LIKE A SMUDGE.**

He journeyed on to the **palace of LIGHT.**

To gain the glow in **mindful SIGHT.**

He studied to be
SMART and bright

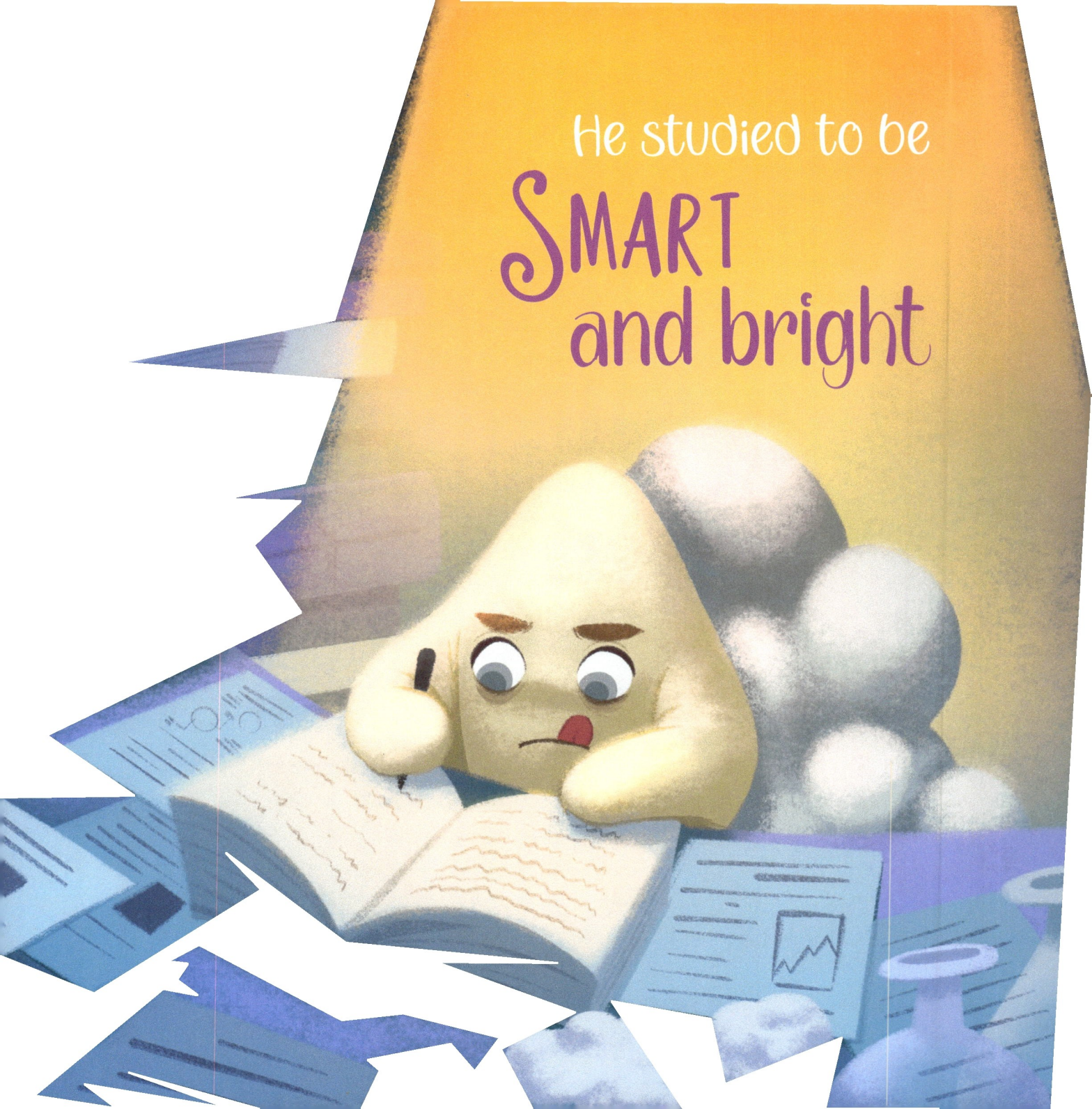

but stayed
INVISIBLE
at night.

On he flew to the **LAST one** that could help.

The man of **SUCCESS,** where **money** prevailed.

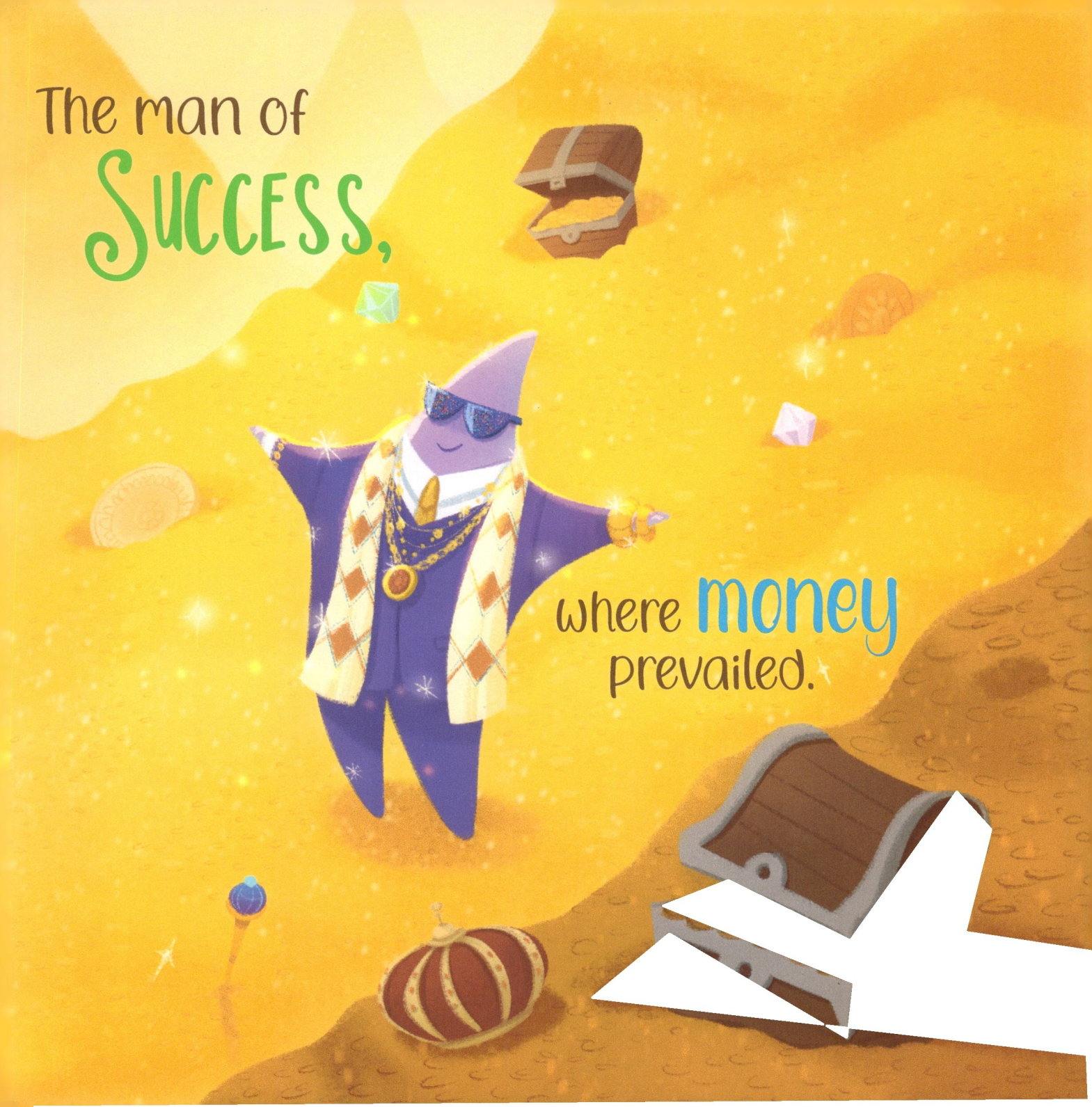

He worked for **endless hours** and **DAYS,**

collected coins and **shiny WAYS.**

Still,
 his heart stayed
 heavy
 and **GREY.**

He missed his *glow* and HAPPY days.

When he was ready to **give UP** and fall, he realized that's what it was, **after ALL.**

"God please grant me the **STRENGTH** to be me. And I shall be **FAITHFUL** and **SHINE** for thee."

A big STORM grabbed him and whirled him around.

He felt he'd been caught by the peace he had found.

Before he knew it
he was HOME
after all,

shining **brighter** than ever

straight from *his soul*.

About the AUTHOR

This former federal criminal detective.
World traveling mother of 5.
Has lived a life full of adversity, triumph,
beauty and perseverance.
Born Nov. 28th 1983 in East Germany behind the wall.
With dreams of one day freely seeing the world.

She would later graduate with an MBA, start her career at the BKA (Bundeskriminalamt). Then in 2010, she resigned and traveled the world. Later moving to Hawaii in 2012, and starting a family.
She likes to say "Have the courage to listen to God".
Only he knows your true purpose.